ONE2ONE

24 studies for
Bible Reading Partnerships

by Andrew Cornes

*For Lance Pierson, whose Bible Reading Partnership with
me laid the foundation of my love for the Bible and
growing understanding of how to understand and apply it.*

The Good Book Company
Elm House, 37 Elm Road
New Malden, Surrey KT3 3HB
Tel: 020-8942-0880; Fax: 020-8942-0990
e-mail: admin@thegoodbook.co.uk
Website: www.thegoodbook.co.uk

ISBN: 1-873166-99-0

Unless otherwise indicated, Scripture quotations in this publication are from the
Holy Bible, English Standard Version. © 2001, Crossway Publishers

Printed in Bilbao, Spain by Grafilur

Typesetting and design by Jon Bradley

ONE2ONE

'Two are better than one, because they have a good reward for their toil'
Ecclesiastes 4:9

These words were originally written for a work context: it is better to work
with someone else than to work alone. The Wisdom Books (Proverbs,
Ecclesiastes, Job, Song of Solomon) have a great deal to say about partnership
and friendship.

For many Christians reading the Bible is hard work. We manage it for a time
and then we give up. Or we keep going without getting much out of our
reading. There can be great gain in meeting regularly to read the Bible with
one other person: a friend or our marriage partner.

A Bible Reading Partnership can revitalise our reading of the Bible: bringing
new insights and keeping us up to the mark. We may well discover that our
reading alone also becomes easier. And it all began when we discovered:
ONE2ONE.

1. **AIM:** The aim is that two Christians should encourage each other as they
    meet regularly to read God's word and talk about what it says. Bible Reading
    Partnerships are no substitute for personal Bible Study (except on the day you
    meet!). At their best, they inspire us to read the Bible more at other times.

2. **PARTNER:** Choose your Bible Reading Partner carefully. If you are married, you
    may want to have your husband / wife as your Bible Reading Partner.
    Otherwise we strongly advise that you choose a partner of your own sex. It
    can be good if a more experienced Christian reads with a person who knows
    their Bible less well.

3. **FREQUENCY:** The ideal is to meet weekly. Some find that it is better for them
    to meet fortnightly. We do not advise meeting less frequently than fortnightly,
    if at all possible.

4. **TIMING:** We suggest that you set aside 90 minutes and keep strictly to whatever timing you have agreed. It is normally a good idea to begin the Bible Study as soon as possible after arrival, and to catch up on news at the end rather than the beginning; experience shows that otherwise the time of Bible Study gets squeezed. One suggestion is: Bible Study 45-60 minutes; Praying Together 5-15 minutes.

5. **STUDYING THE BIBLE:** There are 24 sessions: a passage for each session and questions on it. The aim of these questions is the same as in all genuine study of the Bible: to help us

   • understand what the Bible writer was saying; and
   • apply that message to our lives today.

   You will not always be able to discuss all the questions. That is fine; but make sure you always discuss some of those questions which make you apply the passage to your life today.

6. **PREPARATION:** You will get most out of the Partnership if you study the passage carefully before you meet and note down your answers to the questions. This will undoubtedly make your discussion richer. It is, however, possible to benefit from the Bible Reading Partnership without studying the passage in advance.

7. **VERSION OF THE BIBLE:** The questions occasionally quote from the English Standard Version of the Bible. It is perfectly possible, however, to answer the questions using any other good modern translation.

8. **ORDER:** The 24 sessions are designed to be studied in the following order: John 13-17 (sessions 1-9); Philippians (sessions 10-16); the Psalms (sessions 17-24). This probably provides the best progression. If, however, you wish to go through the sessions in a different order, that is fine.

9   **PRAYING:** It is always good practice to pray **before** we read a passage from the Bible. We want God to speak to us; and it is obvious that we need to ask him to do so.

In addition, there are suggestions for Praying Together at the end of each session. When God has spoken to us, we need to speak in response to him. These suggestions frequently say: 'Pray for each other'. Having discussed and shared together, it is a great encouragement to hear someone else pray about our thoughts / concerns, rather than each of us praying about what we ourselves have mentioned.

As you get to know each other better, it will be very natural of course to pray about other concerns not directly related to the Bible Study. We suggest that you 'pray home' the truths of the passage you have just been reading **before** you pray for other concerns / needs. Otherwise, your and your partner's immediate, pressing needs can edge out the eternal truth you have just been hearing from God.

10   **REVIEW SHEETS:** At the end of each group of sessions there is a review sheet. Please complete this before going on to the next group of sessions. It will help consolidate what you have learned from the Bible.

11   **STARTING AGAIN:** At the end of the course, we hope that you will be able to start again with a new Bible Reading Partner. Your experience will be invaluable to your new partner. In this way, more and more Christians will have the benefits of being involved in a Bible Reading Partnership.

12   **IF IT DOESN'T WORK OUT:** Sometimes a Bible Reading Partnership doesn't fully work. Occasionally the partners don't gel or one partner has to drop out. This is often nobody's fault. We would encourage you to choose a new partner; this new Partnership will very likely go well.

13 FURTHER READING: Some people have asked for reading suggestions to help with these studies. This is not necessary but it can be helpful (as long as you don't make your Bible Reading Partner feel small because they haven't done any extra reading). Here are some suggestions: in each case, the first book is slimmer and the second a little more detailed.

JOHN 13–17		
W. Benn	The Last Word	Christian Focus Publications
B. Milne	The Message of John	IVP
PHILIPPIANS		
W. Barclay	Philippians, Colossians and Thessalonians	St. Andrews Press
J.A. Motyer	The Message of Philippians	IVP
PSALMS		
D. Kidner	The Psalms (2 volumes)	IVP
M. Wilcock	The Message of the Psalms (2 volumes)	IVP

ONE2ONE

Sessions 1-9

John 13 - 17

Jesus' teaching on the
night before he died

Jesus:
Unique and an example to us

Today's passage:

John 13:1-17

When we read the Gospels, it is important to distinguish between two aspects of Jesus' life:

• Where he is Unique. He did things and said things which we could never copy and should never try to. Our job is to understand and worship Jesus in this aspect of his life, not to imitate him.

• Where he is an Example to us. We are his disciples and there is much in his actions and sayings which we are clearly meant to imitate.

This story shows us both aspects of Jesus' life.

A: THE UNIQUE JESUS (read verses 1-11)

1.   What are the tell-tale signs that the foot washing is an 'acted parable' pointing to something unique that Jesus does (v1-11)?

2.   John places this at a particular time and tells us what was on Jesus' mind at that time (v1-3). How do these details help us understand the acted parable?

3.   What was Jesus teaching them about himself through what he did and said in washing their feet (v4-11)?

4   Why were Peter's reactions both inappropriate (v8-9)?
    What appropriate reactions would John want to encourage in us?

B: JESUS OUR EXAMPLE (read verses 12-17)

5   How do we know that in the foot washing Jesus was also setting an example for us to follow (v12-17)?

6   Jesus gives himself two names. What does each name tell us about **why** we should follow Jesus' example (v13-16)?

7   Foot washing was not very pleasant (see v8). Write down at least two somewhat unpleasant ways in which God may be asking you now to care for your fellow Christians.

PRAYING TOGETHER

- Give praise to Jesus that he has made you 'completely clean' (v10).
- Pray for your Bible reading partner that they will have the courage and obedience to care for others in the difficult ways that they have mentioned (see question 7).

Reassurances
from Christ

Today's passage:

John
14:1-14

There are times for all of us when our faith falters. Peter's did (13:36-38). In particular, we may be worried by the thought that:

- there may be no life with Christ after death

- Jesus may not be the only way to God

- Jesus may be no more than a very fine human being

- our prayers aren't really answered

Jesus gives us reassurances ('let not your hearts be troubled' - v1) on all these points.

A: AFTER DEATH (read verses 1-4)

[1] What different reassurances does Christ give that those who believe in him will go to be with him after death (v1-4)?

[2] When have you been 'troubled' (v1) about life after death?
How do these verses encourage you?

B: THE ONLY WAY (read verses 5-7)

[3] Jesus says three things about himself (v6). Explain in your own words the ways in which Jesus is claiming to be unique.

4   Many people today find it offensive that Christ claims to be unique. How would you explain it to a friend?

C: ONE WITH THE FATHER (read verses 8-11)

5   Jesus claimed to be one with the Father. What signs were there, for the disciples to see, that Jesus was one with the Father (v8-11)?

6   When, if ever, do you doubt that Jesus and God the Father are one? Which of these facts (v8-11) do you find most convincing today?

D: ANSWERED PRAYER (read verses 12-14)

7   How do these verses (v12-14) speak to us when we are 'troubled' (v1)?

8   Jesus knew perfectly well that we don't receive everything we ask for (think of his own experience in Gethsemane). So what is he really telling us in verses 12-14?

PRAYING TOGETHER

- Share honestly anything that is troubling you about your Christian faith at the moment.
- Give praise for the reassurances in this passage.

Bible Promises:
then and now

Today's passage:

John
14:15-31

In the Gospels, Jesus made many promises to his disciples. In both Old and New Testaments, God made specific promises to individuals (e.g. Abraham, Paul) and to groups (e.g. Israel, the Church). In reading Scripture, we need to distinguish between promises:

- for then only; e.g. for Abraham and not for us

- for all time; e.g. for all believers

- for then and now but in different ways; e.g. the land of Canaan promised to Abraham through faith and the kingdom of God promised to us through faith

A: RECEIVING THE SPIRIT (read verses 15-17)

1   What does Jesus promise the disciples about the Spirit they will receive (v15-17)?

2   Is there anything which restricts this promise to 'then only', i.e. not to us (v15-17)? If not, how are these verses reassuring to us when we feel 'troubled' (v1, 27)?

B: SEEING JESUS (read verses 18-24)

3   What did Jesus' promises in verses 18-20 mean for the original disciples?

4   Jesus broadens out from the original disciples ('you' in v18-20) to all Christians ('whoever has my commandments' in v21-24). In what ways are the promises to us the same as those to the original disciples, and in what ways are they different (compare v21-24 with v18-20)?

C: BEING TAUGHT BY THE SPIRIT (read verses 25-26)

5   How were these promises fulfilled to the original disciples (v25-26)?

6   How are they fulfilled to us (v25-26)?

D: JESUS' DEPARTURE (read verses 27-31)

7   Why did the original disciples need to hear the teaching and promises of verses 27-31?

8   When would the same promises be an important encouragement to us (v27-31)?

PRAYING TOGETHER

- Which is the promise in this passage which you need to hear most at the moment? Why? Share your answers.
- Pray for each other, that each may trust the promise they have mentioned.

The Parable
of the vine

Today's passage:

John 15:1-11

When reading Gospel Parables, it is important to ask carefully: What was Jesus seeking to teach through this story or word-picture? It is all too easy to read into the parable teaching that is not there (e.g. that Jesus was teaching about his death because the vine's grapes yield wine; or that we need one another because a vine has many branches). Happily, Jesus normally makes quite clear what he is wanting to teach, if we read the parable carefully.

A: THE PARABLE ITSELF (read verses 1-6)

1   In this parable, what is Jesus teaching that **God the Father** does for us Christians (v1-3)? (Note: 'prunes' in verse 2 is, literally, 'cleans').

2   In this parable, what is Jesus teaching that **he (Jesus)** does for us Christians (v3-5)?

3   The parable is full of warnings (v 2,4,5,6). Do they apply to us? If so, what do they teach us?

4   Many passages, like this one, contain both promises and warnings. Which do you think God may be wanting to say most to you at the moment (v1-6)? Why?

B: THE EXTENSION OF THE PARABLE (read verses 7-11)

5   In these verses, Jesus continues with the imagery of the parable (especially in v7-8) but introduces more direct teaching that is no longer in the language of parables (especially in v9-11).
How, in practice, can we 'abide in Christ' (v7-11)

6   How does Jesus' example help us (v9-10)?

7   What practical changes will you make as a result of reading this passage (v1-11)?

PRAYING TOGETHER
- Pray for each other that you will, practically, abide in Christ.
- Pray for each other that you will bear much fruit for God your Father.

Love commanded
and love shown

Today's passage:

John 15:12-17

The disciples were about to lose (the physical presence of) Jesus, who had loved them so much (see verses 12-13. Compare 13:1). They were going to need each other's love all the more.

We need the love of other Christians always, but especially when tragedy strikes.

A: JESUS' LOVE FOR US (read verses 13-16)

1   Although this passage is topped and tailed with the command to love one another (v12, 17), it is mostly about Christ's friendship and love for us. In what ways is Christ's love for us shown (v13-16)?

2   Which of these demonstrations of Christ's love is especially relevant for you at the moment (v13-16)? Why?

B: OUR LOVE FOR FELLOW CHRISTIANS (read verses 12-17)

3   Some people say that love cannot be commanded. Why, then, does Jesus do it
    (v12, 17)?

4   Jesus describes his own love for us (v13-16) in between the commands to love each
    other (v12, 17). What practical suggestions for **how** we can love each other does his
    example give (v12-17)?

5   Who in your Church Family do you need most to learn to love?
    What practical steps are you going to take as a result of reading this passage?

PRAYING TOGETHER

- Pray for each other that you will learn more to appreciate and savour the love of
  Jesus for you.
- Pray for each other that you will put into practice your answers to question 5.

Hatred
from the world

Today's passage:

John 15:18-27

Sometimes we can feel that everybody – our work colleagues, family members, neighbours – is against us. It can lead to self-pity and fear. When the attacks are levelled at our Christian faith, we can feel abandoned by God and left to suffer on our own.

Jesus speaks here to help his disciples (see 16:1); and us.

A: UNDERSTANDING PEOPLE'S HATRED (read verses 18-21)

1 When we're hurt by people's hatred, does it really help us to know that Jesus was hated too (v18, 20-21)? How?

2 In what ways are people around you aware that 'you do not belong to the world' (v19)?

3 Why do people hate you because you are not one of them (v19-21)?

4 How do you normally react when you are treated as an 'outsider' by other people because of your Christian faith?
How does Jesus show, by this teaching, that he wants you to react (v18-21)?

B: UNDERSTANDING PEOPLE'S SIN (read verses 21-25)

5   What constitutes the sin of people who met Jesus (v22-25)?

6   What parts of these verses (21-25) are also true of those who dislike us for our Christian faith today?

7   How did Jesus' teaching in these verses (21-25) help the disciples as they suffered people's hatred? Can we be helped in the same way today? How?

C: UNDERSTANDING THE SPIRIT'S WORK (read verses 26-27)

8   How does the Spirit's work (v26-27) tie in with the hatred we experience from people (v18-25)?

9   In what way will you react differently, as a result of reading this passage, towards those who dislike you (v18-27)?

PRAYING TOGETHER

- Share any ways in which you are currently being cold shouldered, or actively hated, because you are a Christian.
- Pray for each other to react more as Christians to this hatred.
- Pray for Christians in other countries who are hated and attacked.

The blessings
of the Holy Spirit

Today's passage:

John 16:5-15

Deep sadness can blind us to the blessings that God is giving us. The disciples, in their understandable grief at losing Jesus, failed to see that it would actually be better for them (see v6-7). We, when we are sad, can be equally blind to the ways in which God is already blessing us and want to bless us further.

A: THE HOLY SPIRIT AT WORK IN THE WORLD (read verses 8-11)

1. Jesus talks about three things that the Holy Spirit will do to those who are not yet Christians (v8-11). What does each one mean? (Note: ' Sin, righteousness and judgement' is probably **the world's** sin, **Christ's** righteousness and **God's** judgement)

2. How can it be to **our** advantage that the Holy Spirit does these things to non-Christians (v7-11)?

3. In your experience, what evidence have you seen of the Holy Spirit at work in these ways (v8-11)?

B: THE HOLY SPIRIT AT WORK IN CHRISTIANS (read verses 12-15)

4   What was Jesus promising that the Holy Spirit would do for the original disciples (v12-15)?

5   What is Jesus promising here that the Holy Spirit will do for us, twenty first century Christians (v12-15)?

C: THE HOLY SPIRIT AND JESUS (read verses 5-15)

6   How can it possibly be better to have the Holy Spirit than to have Jesus in the flesh beside you (v5-15, especially v7)?

7   What aspect of the Holy Spirit's work has particularly struck you in this passage (v5-15)? Why?

PRAYING TOGETHER

- Which non-Christian (perhaps someone who currently dislikes you – see 15:18-27) would you love to see the Holy Spirit speaking to? Pray together for him/her.
- Pray for each other that the Holy Spirit would lead you to see more of God's truth and Christ's glory.

Jesus' prayer
for his disciples

Today's passage:

John 17:9-19

The twenty first century western world is not at the moment an easy environment in which to be a disciple of Christ. We need all the help we can get from God and through others' prayers, to remain true to God and to our calling as Christians.

Jesus was very conscious that he was leaving his disciples in a hostile environment. 'The hour has come' (v1); he would soon 'no longer be in the world' (v11); he was 'coming to' his Father (v11, 13). It is very instructive to see how he prayed for his disciples.

A: PRAYING FOR THEIR RELATIONSHIP WITH HIM AND THE FATHER
(read verses 9-13)

1. Some of what Jesus says is a statement rather than a prayer. In a hostile environment, what is our relationship to Christ and to the Father (v9-10)?

2. Why do we need what Jesus prayed for his disciples (v11-12)?

3. When have the truths that Jesus has been speaking about and praying about in verses 9-13 given you real joy (v13)?

B: PRAYING FOR THEIR RELATIONSHIP WITH THE WORLD (read verses 14-19)

4. What does Jesus pray for his disciples who are left by him in the world (v14-17)?

5. Why does Jesus pray that God should 'sanctify' them (= make them holy) (v17)? How can 'the truth' make us holy (v17-19)?

6. How do we normally react when people dislike us or put pressure on us to conform? How does Jesus want us to react (v15, 18)?

7. Which part of this prayer do you especially need to ask your Bible Reading Partner to pray for you (v9-19)?

PRAYING TOGETHER
- Give thanks for the firm relationship with Christ that you have been given.
- Pray for each other in line with your answers to question 7.

Jesus' prayer
for us

Today's passage:
John 17:20-26

Some Christians put the emphasis on our relationship with Christ and attach comparatively little importance to our relationship with other Christians (e.g. 'I don't have to go to church very Sunday. I can pray at home'. Or: 'I give the Churches Together Services a wide berth').

Other Christians emphasise our relationship with one another and play down our relationship with Christ (e.g. 'I'm a practical sort of person. I'd rather be giving help to a church member in need than going to a prayer meeting').

Jesus clearly shows, in this last great prayer, that both are important to him.

A: OUR RELATIONSHIP WITH FELLOW CHRISTIANS (read verses 20-23)

1   Jesus turns to pray for later generations of Christians (v20), i.e. us.
What is his overriding concern in prayer for us (v21-23)?
What are the different ways in which he expresses what he wants to see in us (v21-23)?

2   Why does Jesus say that this is so important (v21-23)?

3   What are the barriers in you to unity with all other Christians in your own church?
And how can you respond better to Christ's prayer (v20-23)?

4   What are the barriers in you to unity with other churches in your area?
     And how can you respond better to Christ's prayer (v20-23)?

B: OUR RELATIONSHIP WITH CHRIST AND WITH THE FATHER
(read verses 24-26)

5   What does Jesus pray about our ultimate destiny (v24)?
     Isn't it a rather selfish, almost arrogant, prayer coming from Christ?

6   What does Jesus say about our relationship with him and his Father during our
     lifetime (v25-26)?

7   Which part of Jesus' prayer do you need most to be reminded of (v20-26)? Why?

PRAYING TOGETHER

- Confess those ways in which you have put up barriers to being at one with other
  Christians.
- Thank God for the many Christians you are at one with.
- Praise God for the growing richness of your relationship with him.

Review Sheet
John 13-17

The purposes of this Review Sheet are:

- to help you evaluate your times together
- to make any changes in these times that would make them more helpful
- to consolidate the lessons God has taught you

Discuss your Review with your Bible Reading Partner when you next meet.

How frequently have you normally met?

Weekly ☐   Fortnightly ☐   Once a month ☐   Other ☐

Do you want to meet more frequently?

How long did you normally spend?

Altogether   _____ mins   In Bible Study   _____ mins
In Prayer   _____ mins   In general talking _____ mins

Do you want to change the balance of your time together?

Which sessions on John 13-17 did you find most helpful? Why?

In what ways, if any, have you changed (in your understanding, praying or acting) as a result of studying John 13-17?

In what ways has your Partner helped you as you have read the Bible and prayed together?

ONE2ONE

Sessions 10-16

Philippians

Paul's warm letter to his friends

A warm
and confident beginning

Today's passage:

Philippians
1:1-11

Most of the New Testament is in the form of letters: often written by an apostle to a group of Christians (the Church in a particular city). Probably the best way to understand them is to imagine that you are one of that group of Christians, receiving and reading the letter for the first time. Only when you have understood what Paul was saying to the Philippians can you grasp what God is saying through the letter to you today. If possible, read the whole letter through first.

A: PAUL TO THE PHILIPPIAN CHRISTIANS (read verses 1-2)

1   Paul certainly knew those to whom he was writing (v1-2). Read Acts 16:6-40. What do you think Paul's main memories of his visit to Philippi would have been? Who would be the people that he would be especially remembering as he wrote Philippians 1:1?

B: PAUL'S JOY IN PRAYING FOR THEM (read verses 3-6)

2   Why was Paul able to pray for them with such joy and confidence (v3-6)?

3   Who are the Christians who give you most joy as you pray for them? Why are you able to pray for them with such confidence (v3-6)?

C: PAUL'S FEELINGS TOWARDS THEM (read verses 7-8)

4   Why does Paul feel so positively towards them (v7-8)?

5   Which of your Christian friends could you write the same about (v7-8)?

D: PAUL'S PRAYER FOR THEM (read verses 9-11)

6   What are the different requests in prayer that Paul makes for them (v9-11)?

7   Which of these requests would you most want your Bible Reading Partner to pray for you (v9-11)? Why?

PRAYING TOGETHER

- Thank God for the Christian friends he has given to you and to your Bible Reading Partner.
- Pray for each other in line with your answers to question 7.

Life
and death

Today's passage:

Philippians 1:18b-30

Some parts of the Bible are written to comfort and encourage us. Other parts are written to challenge and confront us. Every part of the Bible is written to change us. The danger is that we can let the Bible wash over us ('Isn't verse 21 wonderful?') without really changing us.

A good example is Paul's attitude to life and death: he would far rather die and leave this earth. Few of us probably would make the same choice. We need therefore to listen carefully to what God says to us through St. Paul, and be changed by it.

A: LIFE AND DEATH (read verses 18b-26)

1 Paul is in prison; he faces possibly execution. What are his hopes for his trial (v18b-20)?

2 How do you hope that 'Christ will be honoured in your body' in the week ahead (v18b-20)?

3 What, for Paul, are the different advantages of remaining alive and of dying (v21-26)?

4   Why does Paul prefer one of these prospects (v21-23)?
Why is he convinced that God will give him the other (v22-26)?

5   How has reading this passage changed your view of this life and / or of death (v18b-26)?

B: LIFE IN THE CHURCH (read verses 27-30)

6   What does Paul especially want for the Philippian Christians (v27-28)?

7   In what ways are we to react to opposition to our Christian faith (v27-30)?

8   In what practical ways could you 'strive side by side with others for the faith of the gospel' (v27-30, especially v27)?

PRAYING TOGETHER

- Give thanks that, if we are Christians, we are with Christ after death.
- Pray for each other in line with your answers to question 8.

Humility
and love

Today's passage:

Philippians
2:1-11

When we become Christians, we are brought into the Family of Christ. Christians, therefore, spend a lot of time together. This has enormous advantages: it gives us friendship, support, opportunities to serve. But it also has a downside: it can lead to friction, falling out with one another, promoting the interests of our own circle of Christian friends. These tensions were there in the Philippian Church; they have been present in every Church from the 1st century to the 21st. Paul's teaching here is vitally relevant and helpful to us.

A: FOCUS ON CHRIST (read verses 1-8)

1. Paul puts Christ forward as our example. Trace the various steps down that Jesus took (v5-8) and show how each step was an example of one or more of the principles in verses 1-4.

2. Which of the decisions which Christ took do you admire most (v5-8)? Why?

B: FOCUS ON US (read verses 1-8)

3   How would your Christian life be different if you put into practice verses 1-4?

4   Paul tells us to have the same mind as Christ's (v5). How in practice can we learn to think like Christ (v5-8) when our natural reaction is to be self centred (v1-4)?

5   Which one of the positive commands in verses 2-4 do you most need to concentrate on? What specific action will you take to fulfil it?

C: FOCUS ON GOD'S REACTION (read verses 1-11)

6   How does God react to Christ's steps down (v5-11)?

7   Why does Paul include verses 9-11 in the whole passage (v1-11)?

PRAYING TOGETHER

• Thank Christ for what he did for us (especially thinking of your answers to question 2).
• Pray for each other to learn unselfish love, in line with your answers to question 5.

Growing
as a Christian

Today's passage:

Philippians
2:12-18

Someone has said: 'The Christian life is like riding a bicycle. If you're not going forward, you're falling off'. Of course our growth as a Christian is faster and more evident in our earlier years as a Christian. Nevertheless, I should always be able to say: 'I am a more consistent Christian than I was a year ago'. As you read this passage, ask yourself whether you have **grown** in each area in the last year.

A: WORKING OUT (read verses 12-13)

1   What do you think Paul means by the phrase: 'working out your own salvation with fear and trembling' (v12)? In what ways are you already doing this?

2   It is always easier to work on your Christian life 'in the presence' of Christians you look up to. How do you ensure that you continue to 'work out your salvation' when you are away from other Christians (v12)?

3   In what ways are you conscious that verse 13 is true in your life?

B: STANDING OUT (read verses 14-16)

4   How does Paul say we can be different from the world around us (v14-16)?

5   In what situations do you tend to 'grumble' (v14)?
How thoughts in this passage would have the power to stop you?

What thoughts in this passage would have the power to stop you?

C: POURING OUT (read verses 16-18)

6   Why was Paul so passionately concerned for the Philippians' faith (v16-18)?
Isn't that rather selfish?

7   What was Paul willing to do, and how would that help the Philippians (v17-18)?

8   What is the greatest sacrifice that God is (or: may be) asking you to make at the
moment (v17-18)?

PRAYING TOGETHER

- Thank God for the ways that he is already at work in your lives.
- Pray for each other to take practical steps to grow spiritually, especially in line with your answers to questions 1 and 2.
- Pray for each other that you will be willing to make the sacrifices God will ask of you this month.

Life
goals

Today's passage:

Philippians 3:2-14

All of us have goals in life. Often we have never stated them clearly. Often we picked them up quite unconsciously from our parents, our closest friends at school, the ethos of the place where we work or the people we mix with. They determine most of our basic attitudes and where we focus our energies. Yet precisely because we may not be fully conscious of them, we may not have overhauled them in the light of Christ. Paul, in this autobiographical passage, shows how radically God had changed his life goals.

A: PREVIOUS GOALS (read verses 2-9)

1. Paul is writing against strict Jews who are insisting that Gentile Christians should be circumcised and follow Jewish practices (v2-3). Paul had been a strict Jew himself. List all the things he had once thought important (v2-9).

2. What is the nearest equivalent in your personal upbringing and past life to each of the items on this list (v2-9)?

3. How did Paul come to regard these things and what made him change his mind (v2-4, 7-9)?

4   Are there things from your upbringing and past life which you still regard fondly or are proud of but which need to be viewed quite differently in the light of Christ (v2-9)?

B: PRESENT GOALS (read verses 7-11)

5   What were Paul's present goals in life (v7-11)?

6   Which of Paul's goals can you say are already yours (v7-11)? What steps do you need to take to accept fully any of Paul's goals which are not yet yours (v7-11)?

C: CURRENT PROGRESS (read verses 12-14)

7   Paul states clearly that he has not yet reached his goal (v12-13). What steps does he take to ensure that he is getting closer all the time (v12-14)?

8   'Forgetting what lies behind' and 'Straining forward to what lies ahead' (v13). Which do you think is more important for you, and why? What in practice will you do to make it a reality?

PRAYING TOGETHER

- Pray for each other, in line with your answers to question 4, that you will be able fully to reject previous un-Christian goals.
- Pray for each other that you will be able fully to embrace the Christian goals of this passage.

Let peace
reign

Today's passage:

Philippians
4:2-9

Verses 2-3 give a glimpse of Church life at Philippi. When we read this, or when we (more frequently) read historical incidents in the Gospels, Acts or Old Testament Historical Books, a very helpful way to understand and apply them is to identify with one of the characters. It is perfectly possible, and legitimate, to identify with several in turn.

As an example, we can ask ourselves on verses 2-3:

both • How am I like Euodia and Syntyche who were arguing?

and • How can I be like Paul's 'true companion' (v3) and help Christians I know who are at loggerheads?

A: DISAGREEMENTS IN THE CHURCH (read verses 2-3)

1 Have you fallen out with any fellow Christian?
If so, what practical steps must you take to obey these verses (v2-3)?

2 Do you know other Christians who have fallen out with each other?
If so, what practical steps should you take to 'help them' to be reconciled (v2-3)?

3 Why does Paul mention the women's past involvement in ministry (v3)?

B: BRIEF THOUGHTS (read verses 4-7)

4   Paul gives several brief commands / thoughts in verses 4-7. Which is most important for you at the present time? Why?

5   Most Christians admit they are worriers and are often not fully at peace. What is the key thought for you in verses 6-7? What steps must you take to put it into practice?

C: THINKING ALONG THE RIGHT LINES (read verses 8-9)

6   At what times do you find your thoughts turning naturally to good things (v8-9)?

7   At what times do you find your thoughts turning naturally to bad things? What must you do to change your thoughts at those times (v8-9)?

8   What is the connection between verse 9 and verse 8?

PRAYING TOGETHER

- Pray for each other that you will resolutely seek reconciliation with any Christian who has hurt or angered you.
- Pray for each other that you will take the practical steps that will drive out worry.
- Pray for each other that your thoughts will be increasingly in tune with Christ.

Money
and lifestyle

Today's passage:

Philippians
4:10-20

Money is probably the hardest area over which to trust God. For most of us, our upbringing, training and natural instincts combine to tell us:

• you cannot be happy without money

• you cannot be secure without savings (and when we have them, we feel we need more)

• you would be foolish to give away any significant percentage of your money

There is wisdom in all these attitudes, but it is worldly wisdom; and normally it hasn't been re-thought and re-fashioned in the light of Christ's love and God's kingship. This passage encourages us to make that re-evaluation.

A: BEING CONTENT WITH ANY LIFESTYLE (read verses 10-13)

1   Did Paul know what he was talking about in verses 11-13? (Try to answer this from specific events / incidents you know already from the life of St. Paul. If you get stuck, read 2 Corinthians 11:23-33 and try to tie in what he says there with these verses in Philippians.)

2   What was the 'secret' that Paul had 'learned' (v10-13)?

3   In what ways will you be helped to learn this same secret, whatever your financial situation or standard of living (v10-13)?

B: GENEROUS GIVING (read verses 10, 14-20)

4 What did the Philippians' generous giving do for Paul (v10, 14-18)?
   Have you experienced the same when people have given generously to you?

5 What effects did the Philippians' generous giving have on them (v10, 15-19)?
   Have you experienced the same when you have given generously?

6 How does God react to our generous giving (v18-20)?
   Do you in practice find God's reactions an incentive to give? Why?

7 What practical changes must you make to your financial goals, and to your giving, in order to put this whole passage into practice (v10-20)?

PRAYING TOGETHER

- Pray for each other that you will take the steps to learn contentment which you mentioned in answer to question 3.
- Pray for each other that you will make the changes in your financial goals, and your giving, which you talked about in answer to question 7.

Review Sheet
Philippians

The purposes of this Review Sheet are:

- to help you evaluate your times together
- to make any changes in these times that would make them more helpful
- to consolidate the lessons God has taught you

Discuss your Review with your Bible Reading Partner when you next meet.

How frequently have you normally met?

Weekly ☐ Fortnightly ☐ Once a month ☐ Other ☐

Do you want to meet more frequently?

How long did you normally spend?

Altogether	_____ mins	In Bible Study	_____ mins
In Prayer	_____ mins	In general talking	_____ mins

Do you want to change the balance of your time together?

Which sessions on Philippians did you find most helpful? Why?

In what ways, if any, have you changed (in your understanding, praying or acting) as a result of studying Philippians together?

Philippians was written to a Church. What are the most important lessons in what you have read for your Church? How in practice could you help these lessons for your Church become a reality?

ONE2ONE

Sessions 17-24

The Psalms

The Best Worship Book
on the Market

One man's experience
and everyone's

Today's passage:

Psalm 22:1-24

Many of the Psalms record the particular experiences of the person who wrote them. Yet because God is the same, and human nature is the same, we may have similar experiences today, which is why the Psalms have been such a help and encouragement to Christians down the ages.

So the Psalms operate on two levels: the experience of the individual writer (or of the nation of Israel) and the experience of all Christian people.

There are also some Psalms, of which this is one, which operate on a third level: they are a prophecy of Christ. In fact, most Old Testament prophecy (whether in the Psalms, the Prophets' writings or other books containing prophecies, e.g. Genesis) operates on at least two levels: with a specific message for the people of the writer's own day and a wider message for Israelites, and then Christians, down the ages. Often they operate also on the third level: as a specific prophecy of Christ.

We will be exploring all three levels of Psalm 22.

A: THE WRITER'S PARTICULAR EXPERIENCE (read verses 1-21)

1. What things did the writer find so painful in his relationship with God (v1-21)?

2. What did the writer find painful about the ways he was treated by other humans (v6-21)?

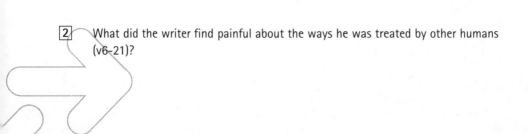

B: CHRIST'S EXPERIENCE (read verses 1-21)

3   What are the detailed historical events of the Crucifixion which are prophesied here (v1-21)?

4   What insights, if any, does this Psalm give us into how Christ was probably feeling as he faced up to, and then experienced, death on the Cross (v1-21)?

C: OUR EXPERIENCE (read verses 1-21)

5   When, if ever, have you known the same kinds of pain in your relationship with God (v1-21)?

6   When, if ever, have you known the same kinds of hurtful treatment from other humans (v6-21)?

D: GOD'S RESPONSE (read verses 21-24)

7   How did God respond to the writer (v21-24)? To Christ in his agony (v21-24)?
To you, when you have been in deep pain (v21-24)?

PRAYING TOGETHER

- Pray for each other in any pain you are going through, or have been through, because you have been forsaken by humans or have seemed to be forsaken by God.
- Give praise to Christ for the agony he went through for you.

The Shepherd
and the host

Today's passage:

Psalm 23

The Bible is, of course, full of picture language: using pictures from everyday life to teach us truths about God and ourselves. The most famous form of picture language is the Parable teaching of Jesus. Psalm 23 is perhaps the best known example in the Old Testament.

But in understanding and applying the Bible's picture language, there are two things we need to watch:

- The Bible often changes picture quite suddenly. Here the picture of God as Shepherd (v1-4) changes to God as Host at a Victory Feast (v5-6)

- We must not push the Bible's picture language beyond what it actually says. It is not legitimate to say: 'A Shepherd in the East walked in front of his sheep; therefore God goes before us into all life's situations'; this Psalm uses the picture of God as Shepherd and makes several points from the picture, but not the one just quoted. We must stick to what the Bible actually teaches in its use of the picture.

A: GOD AS SHEPHERD (read verses 1-4)

1. What are the different ways in which the Shepherd is pictured as caring for the sheep (v1-4)? What does each of these tell us about God?

2. Which of these aspects of God's shepherding do you need especially to be reassured about at the moment (v1-4)? Why?

B: GOD AS HOST (read verses 5-6)

[3] How has the picture changed in these verses? How are we described (v5-6)? How is God described (v5-6)?

[4] What kind of 'enemies' do you have now, or have you known in the past (v5)? Is the picture of what God does in verse 5 something which you have in fact experienced? How?

[5] How did the Psalmist respond to God's goodness (v6)? What is the equivalent response for Christians today?

[6] If you could pick out one part of this Psalm through which God has spoken to you today, which would it be (v1-6)? Why?

PRAYING TOGETHER

- Thank God for the way he acts towards you as both Shepherd and Host.
- Thank him for how he has spoken to you today through this Psalm, in line with your answers to questions 2 and 6.

Forgiveness

Today's passage:

Psalm 32

It is quite common in the Psalms and the Books of the Prophets, which are mostly written in Hebrew poetry, for the person speaking to change several times in one chapter. The change is normally quite clear if you look carefully at the chapter; and it is important to grasp what is going on so that we can understand God's teaching for us. In Psalm 32:

- In verses 1 and 2 the Writer addresses us (his readers) and speaks about God in the third person ('the Lord' - verse 2)

- In verses 3-7 the Writer (who calls himself 'I') addresses God ('you') and speaks about his readers in the third person ('him' - verse 6)

- In verses 8-9 God (who calls himself 'I') addresses the Writer ('you')

- In verses 10-11 the Writer returns to the format of verses 1-2: he addresses us his readers ('you') and speaks about God in the third person ('the Lord')

This is quite frequent in the Old Testament, and we often make the adjustment of viewpoint without realising it.

A: FORGIVENESS FOR THE PAST (read verses 1-5)

1. What happens when we don't admit to our sin (v1-4)? (Note: 'I kept silent' (v3) means: 'I kept silent about my sin')

2. What are the benefits when we do admit to our sin (v1-5)?

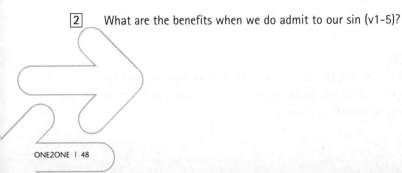

$\boxed{3}$ When have you experienced what this passage says happens:
- when we don't admit to our sin (v1-4)?
- when we do admit to our sin (v1-5)?

B: GOD'S RESPONSE (read verses 6-11)

$\boxed{4}$ This next section is clearly linked to the last (v6: 'Therefore'). What does God promise us (through the writer's comments: 6-7, 10-11; and through God's direct speaking: v8-9) when we have faced up to our sin (v6-11)?

$\boxed{5}$ When in the past has your experience echoed the words of verses 6-7?

$\boxed{6}$ In what areas now do you need to hear the encouragement and warning of verses 8-9?

$\boxed{7}$ Why does the writer add verses 10-11 to a Psalm about forgiveness of sin (1-11)? Is the contrast in verse 10 true to your experience?

PRAYING TOGETHER
- Pray for each other that you will be able honestly to admit to your sin (perhaps leave a few minutes to do this silently).
- Thank God for the joy, protection and guidance he gives when we do admit to our sins and they are forgiven.

Longing
for God

Today's passage:

Psalm 42

What do you do when for a long time God seems to have been far from you? Do you give up altogether, feeling that you're not getting anything out of your Christian life – or at least out of Sunday worship – so there's no point continuing with it? Do you lower your expectations and keep going? Do you reassure yourself that every Christian goes through dry months?

This Psalm shows the problem clearly and points the way forward.

A: WHERE IS MY GOD (read verses 1-11)?

1   What are the phrases which show you how painful the Psalmist's present experience is (v1-11)? When, if ever, have you felt the same way?

2   How do other people make matters worse (v3-10)?
Have you found sometimes that people have twisted the knife in the wound when you have felt far from God (v3-10)?

3   Twice the writer says he 'remembers' (v4, 6). Do these thoughts make matters better or worse (v4-8)?

(**Note:** The places mentioned in verse 6 are quite a long way from the Temple which is mentioned in verse 4 as 'the house of God').

B: LONGING FOR MY GOD (read verses 1-11)

[4]   How, apart from in a cry of pain, does the Psalmist react to God's absence (v1-11)?

[5]   Do you think the end of verse 5 and of verse 11 express fundamental confidence or is he trying vainly to convince himself it will be all right in the end? Why (v1-11)?

[6]   How does verse 8 fit in the Psalm (v1-11)?

[7]   If you are feeling that God is far from you at the moment, what does this Psalm especially say to you and what will you do about it (v1-11)?
Or: If a friend told you that (s)he had for a long time felt that God was miles away, what one thing would you want to show him/her from this Psalm (v1-11)?

PRAYING TOGETHER

- Give thanks to God if he has in the past brought you out of a long period of feeling he was far from you.
- Pray for each other or for any friend if you/the friend feel(s) God is far away at the moment.
- Pray that you will be able sensitively to help any friends who feel that God is far away.

Everything
out of perspective

Today's passage:

Psalm 73

In Psalm 42 (which you studied in the last session), the writer was thinking almost entirely about God: how God had been very close to him and was now so far away. In Psalm 73, the writer thinks initially only about the godless people around him and gets depressed as he compares his life with theirs.

A: FALSE PERSPECTIVE (read verses 2-14)

1. What different facts made the comparison between the life of the writer and of the godless so dispiriting (v2-14)?

2. What did the writer feel about his own life of obedience to God (v11-14)?

3. When have you found yourself thinking in the same way (v2-14)?

B: THE TURNING POINT (read verses 15-20)

4. What proved to be the turning point for the writer (v15-17)?

[5]   How did he come to view his own previous feelings (v15-17)? Why?

[6]   How did he come to view the people he had envied (v18-20)?
Is this a Christian way of looking at people we envy (v18-20)? Why/why not?

C: TRUE PERSPECTIVE (read verses 1, 21-28)

[7]   How did the writer come to think about himself (v21-22, 27-28)?

[8]   How did he come to think about God (v1, 23-28)

[9]   What do you think is the most important verse in this Psalm for you at the moment (v1-28)? Why?

PRAYING TOGETHER

- Confess to God the envy you sometimes feel for those who are not Christians.
- Pray for each other that God will give you a true perspective on your life and the life of those you envy.
- Pray for each other in line with your answers to question 9.

Church
and nation

Large parts of the Old Testament are about God's dealings with Israel, his warnings to Israel and his promises to Israel. How are we to apply these parts of Scripture today?

- The Church is the modern equivalent of Israel. God calls Israel 'my people' (see verses 2,6,8); the people of God today are the members of the Christian Church. The New Testament often takes Old Testament promises made to Israel and applies them to the Church. This is clearly a legitimate way to apply with care many parts of the Old Testament where God is dealing with Israel. But also:

- A Nation (particularly one which claims in any way to be Christian) is the modern equivalent of Israel. In the Old Testament Israel is frequently viewed more as a nation state than a worshipping community (e.g. the promise of economic success in verse 12). God deals with nations as well as individuals and many chapters of the Old Testament Prophets speak of his dealings with nations other than Israel; so does the New Testament Book of Revelation. To apply Scripture cautiously to your national life is, then, a legitimate way to think about many parts of the Old Testament where God is dealing with Israel.

A: GOD AND ISRAEL (read verses 1-13)

1. What different reactions did God have to Israel at different stages (v1-7)? Can you think of periods in Israel's history which show these different reactions (v1-7)?

2. What promises does God make to Israel (v8-13)?

3. God promises that four things will meet in verse 10 (two are repeated in verse 11). What exactly could Israel expect from God as a result of these promises (v10-11)?

4   Are God's promises conditional on any response from the Israelites (v8-13)? If so, what are the conditions?

B: GOD AND THE CHURCH (read verses 1-13)

5   Which of the reactions in this Psalm is God now showing to his Church in your country (v1-13)? Why (v1-13)? Are you experiencing the same reaction of God in your own church (v1-13)? Why (v1-13)?

6   Can the Church in your country expect the same future that God promises in this Psalm (v8-13)? Why/why not (v1-13)?

C: GOD AND THE NATION (read verses 1-13)?

7   Which of the reactions in this Psalm is God now showing to your nation (v1-13)? Why (v1-13)?

8   Can your nation expect any of the same future that God promises in this Psalm (v8-13)? Why/why not (v1-13)?

PRAYING TOGETHER

- Pray for the Church in your country that God will 'revive us again' (v6).
- Pray for your nation that God will 'give what is good' (v12).

God's
steadfast love

Today's passage:

Psalm 107:1-22

This is a celebration of God's unfailing, committed love. Israel saw it particularly in the late 6th Century BC when the scattered exiles (after the destruction of Jerusalem by Nebuchadnezzar in 587BC) were suddenly given the opportunity to return (see v2-3). We may apply it especially to our conversion (when the way to God was first opened up to us) and/or to more recent ways in which we have been helped and rescued from harm.

It **may** be that the Psalmist thought literally of people in deserts (v4), prison (v10) and sickness (v17-18), but it is at least as likely that he intended this as picture language; we are **like** those in deserts, prison or sickness.

A: RESCUED FROM THE DESERT (read verses 1-9)

1   What were these people like before God helped them (v4-5)? Does this language describe some of your experiences before or after becoming a Christian (v4-5)?

2   What proved the turning point (v6)? When has the same act proved a turning point for you (v6)?

3   What did God do for them (v7-9)? Does this language describe some of what God has done for you (v7-9)? Please explain.

B: RESCUED FROM PRISON (read verses 10-16)?

4   What were these people like before God helped them (v10-13)? Does this language describe some of your experiences before or after becoming a Christian (v10-13)?

5   What does God do for prisoners who cry to him (v14-16)? Could you use this language for what God has done for you (v14-16)? Please explain.

C: RESCUED FROM SICKNESS (read verses 17-22)?

6   What was happening to these people before God helped them (v17-19)? Does this language describe experiences of yours at any stage in your life (v17-19)?

7   What did God do for them (v19-20)? Has God done the same for you either literally or in a spiritual sense (v19-20)? Please explain.

8   What are the reactions of the people whom God had helped (v1-22)? What helps you in practice to continue reacting in the same way (v1-22)?

PRAYING TOGETHER

- Using the language of this Psalm, give thanks for how God rescued you when you were first led to Christ.
- Using the language of this Psalm, give thanks for ways in which God has rescued you since your conversion to Christ.

The Vital Importance
of God's word

Today's passage:

Psalm 119:1-16

It seems appropriate that in the last session of your Bible Reading Partnership you should be studying what the Psalms say about the Bible. Psalm 119 is the longest chapter in the Bible (176 verses!) and almost every verse includes some expression meaning God's revealed truth (e.g. law, testimonies, ways, precepts, statutes, commandments, rules, word). For the Psalmist, God's revealed truth was written down in those books of the Bible which had by then been produced. For us God's word is the whole Bible, both Old and New Testaments. Psalm 119 is written in 22 stanzas (or paragraphs). We will be exploring the first two (verses 1-16).

A: THE OPENING STANZA (read verses 1-8)

1   What does the Bible do for those who take it seriously (v1-8)?

2   Have those things been true in your recent experience of reading the Bible (v1-8)? Please explain.

3   What do these verses tell us we should do with the Bible (v1-8)?
What specific steps can you take to put these ideas into practice (v1-8)?

B: THE SECOND STANZA (read verses 9-16)

4   What further things does the Bible do for those who take it seriously (v9-16)?

5   Some of these verses are prayers. What can we learn from them about how to pray meaningfully for our own Bible reading (v9-16)?

6   What do these verses tell us we should do with the Bible (v9-16)?
What specific steps can you take to put these ideas into practice (v9-16)?

7   How can you ensure that you 'will not forget God's word' (v16)?

C: WHERE DO YOU GO FROM HERE?

8   Read the next page of this book: 'Where do we go from here?' What do you think the next step for you will be? Write it down here; and then discuss it with your partner.

PRAYING TOGETHER

- Give thanks to God for the Bible, for what he promises to give us through it and for what you have experienced of the Bible together.
- Pray for each other that you will continue to read God's word regularly.
- Pray for each other about your future involvement in Bible Reading Partnerships, in line with your answers to question 8.

Review Sheet
The Psalms

The purposes of this Review Sheet are:

- to help you evaluate your times together
- to make any changes in these times that would make your next Bible Reading Partnership more helpful
- to consolidate the lessons God has taught you

How frequently have you normally met?

Weekly ☐   Fortnightly ☐   Once a month ☐   Other ☐

Would you want in your next Bible Reading Partnership to meet more frequently?

How long did you normally spend?

Altogether	_____ mins	In Bible Study	_____ mins
In Prayer	_____ mins	In general talking	_____ mins

Would you want to change the balance of time in your next Bible Reading Partnership?

Which sessions on the Psalms did you find most helpful? Why?

In what ways, if any, has your attitude to God, and your worship of God, changed as a result of reading these Psalms?

In what ways has your Partner helped you as you have read the Bible and prayed together?

Where do we go from here?

▷ Our hope is that an increasing number of Christians will be involved in, and benefit from, Bible Reading Partnerships. If you have enjoyed and gained from the Partnership which has just finished, we imagine that you share that hope.

▷ If so, you can help to fulfil this vision. Rather than staying with the same Bible Reading Partner – which would be comfortable but would not spread the benefits of Bible Partnerships – choose a new Bible Reading Partner of your own sex and start again.

▷ In this new Partnership, you can be the more experienced Christian and share with someone who will gain from being your partner.

▷ You may think that it will be dull going over the same material. Experience shows that it will be a totally new experience. The Bible itself doesn't change, but your new Bible Reading Partner will bring different insights, and you will have moved on as well. We recommend that you obtain a new copy of this book and write down your answers to the questions afresh. This will ensure that you continue to gain new insights.

▷ You will need to be willing to change down a few gears. You probably remember that your present Partnership took some weeks to get going. You must expect the same with your new Partnership. It may be a little sticky at first but you will gradually grow in friendship and mutual trust. A new and equally valuable Partnership will blossom little by little.

▷ Not everyone, of course, will want to begin a new Partnership; some will want to take a break, at least for a while. But we hope that you will be willing to begin in the near future with a new Partner and discover all over again the value of ONE2ONE.

Where do you go from here?

▷ Do you want to start again with a new Bible Reading Partner?   **YES / NO**

▷ If so, when would you like to start? _____

▷ Whom would you invite to be your next Bible Reading Partner (perhaps a less experienced Christian of your own sex)? _____

More great Bible study resources from
The Good Book Company

short steps for long gains
Short Bible studies

This small booklet has been written to provide a focus for Christians who meet together briefly and regularly to look at God's Word, pray and share something of their lives. The 26 short studies make up an introductory A to Z of Christian living, providing weekly reflections for half a year, or a year's fortnightly input.   **Price: £1.00**

explore
Bible notes for adults

Explore is written by people who share a passion for getting the Bible to work in people's lives. Each issue contains 90 daily readings with ideas for further reading, prayer and practical points to ponder, to help you understand clearly the message and challenge of God's word.

Sample issue: £1.00
Single issue: £2.50
Annual Subscription (UK): £10.00

on the move
Bible readings for people on the go

This is the first of an experimental format for a daily Bible-reading resource for commuters and others who may not have the time for a quiet time at home. It combines the printed text of the passage to be studied with a brief introduction and a couple of questions to ponder and apply. There are also brief suggestions for prayer. Each booklet contains forty readings—enough for two months-worth of train journeys to work! The first issue contains readings on Mark and Ephesians.